SAVING WILDLIFE

Grassland Animals

Sonya Newland

FRANKLIN WATTS
LONDON•SYDNEY

This edition 2014

Franklin Watts
338 Euston Road
London NW1 3BH

Franklin Watts Australia
Level 17/207 Kent Street
Sydney NSW 2000

Produced for Franklin Watts by

White-Thomson Publishing
+44 (0)843 208 7460
www.wtpub.co.uk

Series consultant: Sally Morgan
Designer: Clare Nicholas
Picture researcher: Amy Sparks

A CIP catalogue record for this book is available from the British Library.

ISBN (pb): 978 1 4451 3656 1
ISBN (Library ebook): 978 1 4451 2216 8

Dewey Classification: 591.7'4

Picture Credits
Dreamstime: Cover (Mhpiper); **Nature Picture Library:** 25b (Mark Carwardine), Photolibrary: 6 (Steve Turner), 10 (John Warburton-Lee), 13b (Ariadne Van Zandbergen), 17t (Jeff Vanuga), 18 (Heinz Plenge), 19t (Juniors Bildarchiv), 19b (John Cancalosi), 21 (Alan and Joan Root), 25t (Geoff Higgins), 27b (Tom Ulrich); **Shutterstock:** 4 (Paul Banton), 6-7 (Dusan Po), 8 (Chris Kruger), 9t (Karel Gallas), 9b (Johan Swanepoel), 11t (Eduardo Rivero), 11b (photobar), 12 (Sam DCruz), 13t (Maxim Kulko), 14 (Lee Prince), 15t (Paul Banton), 15b (Will Davies), 16 (Peter Kirillov), 17b (Arto Hakola), 20t (Mogens Trolle), 20b (Gilmanshin), 22l (Susan Flashman), 22r (Sam DCruz), 23t (Christian Musat), 24l (WORAKIT), 24r (Near and Far Photography), 26 (Andrejs Jegorovs), 27t (Jim Parkin); **US Fish & Wildlife Service:** 23b.

Every attempt has been made to clear copyright. Should there be any inadvertent omissions, please apply to the publisher for rectification.

Printed in China

Franklin Watts is a division of Hachette Children's Books, an Hachette UK Company.
www.hachette.co.uk

Contents

Words in **bold** are in the glossary on page 31.

Grassland Habitats

Around a quarter of our planet's land is grassland. These are large areas that receive just enough rainfall for grasses to grow, but not enough for a lot of trees and other plants to thrive.

Where are grasslands?

Grasslands usually lie between deserts and mountains. There are two main types of grassland. Tropical grasslands lie close to the **Equator**, and include the African savannah. Temperate grasslands are cooler and further from the Equator, such as the North American prairies and the pampas of South America. Steppe is the coldest but driest type of temperate grassland, found in countries such as Russia, China and Mongolia.

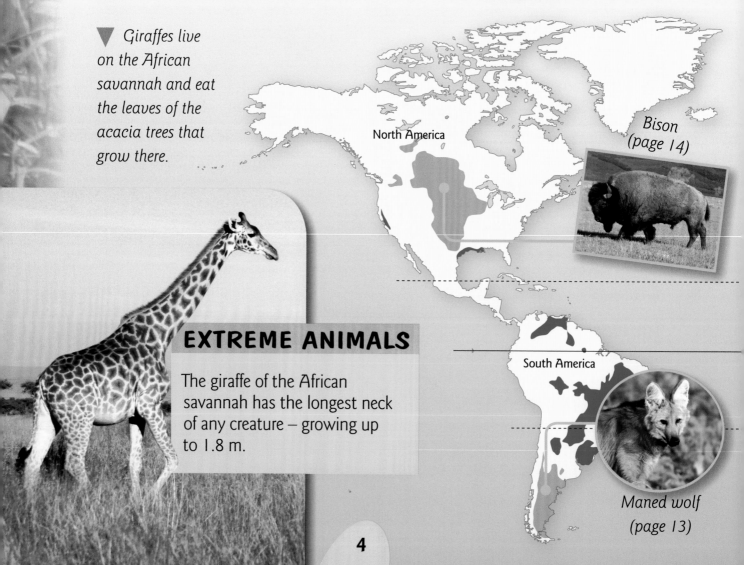

▼ *Giraffes live on the African savannah and eat the leaves of the acacia trees that grow there.*

North America

Bison (page 14)

South America

EXTREME ANIMALS

The giraffe of the African savannah has the longest neck of any creature – growing up to 1.8 m.

Maned wolf (page 13)

Animals in the grass

It might seem as though there is not much life in these huge expanses of land, but among the tall grasses, large and small creatures exist in a complex web of life. The grasses provide food for grazing animals such as antelope and zebras. In turn, these grazing animals are food for **predators** such as big cats and wild dogs. Other creatures keep the **habitat** healthy for themselves and other animals. Burrowing animals, such as prairie dogs, create tunnels that allow air into the soil. Waste from larger animals provides **nutrients** that keep the soil healthy. Many animals are now **endangered**, though, and this is threatening the balance of the grassland **ecosystem**.

▼ This map shows the world's grassland areas. Among the largest are the savannahs of Africa.

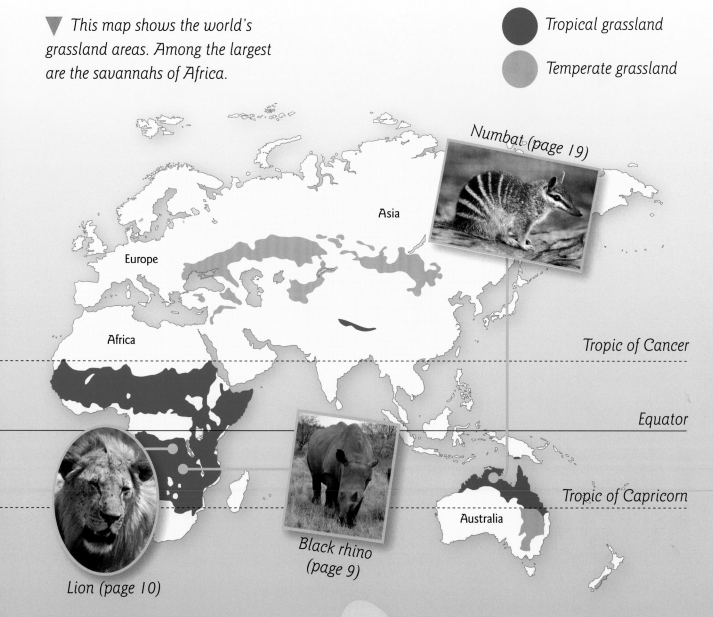

Tropical grassland

Temperate grassland

Numbat (page 19)

Asia

Europe

Africa

Tropic of Cancer

Equator

Tropic of Capricorn

Australia

Black rhino (page 9)

Lion (page 10)

Grasslands Under Threat

Some of the world's most amazing and majestic animals live in grasslands, but many of them are in danger of dying out because of human activity.

Human hunters

Hunting has long been a threat to grassland animals. In Africa, **big game** hunters killed large numbers of animals such as lions, elephants and rhinos simply for sport. Although hunting is strictly controlled now, some creatures are still **poached** illegally because their meat, fur or **ivory** tusks are valuable.

Human settlement

More and more grassland areas are being taken over by people so they can live there, build roads or farm the land. Most prairie land in the USA, for example, has now been turned into farmland. This has driven away the large animals that used to roam there freely, such as wolves and bison. In some countries, people are searching for oil in grassland areas. This can affect the quality of the soil, cause **fragmentation** and destroy animal habitats.

These elephant tusks were taken away from poachers in Kenya, Africa. Today, hunting elephants is banned.

ENDANGERED ANIMALS

The International Union for Conservation of Nature (IUCN, see page 28) lists animals according to how endangered they are.

Extinct: Died out completely.

Extinct in the wild: Only survive in captivity.

Critically endangered: Extremely high risk of becoming extinct in the near future.

Endangered: High risk of becoming extinct in the wild.

Vulnerable: High risk of becoming endangered in the wild.

Near threatened: Likely to become endangered in the near future.

Least concern: Lowest risk of becoming endangered.

The warming world

Climate change is affecting grassland areas too. Experts think that changes in the pattern of rainfall may cause vital watering holes to dry up. If this happens, deserts could gradually spread into grassland areas.

▼ *In many countries in Europe, as well as in the USA, grassland areas have been taken over for use as farmland.*

WHAT DO YOU THINK?

Grasslands are being taken over to meet human needs. What compromises could be made that would reduce the impact on grassland wildlife?

Giants in the Grass

The large animals that roam the African savannah are some of the most familiar creatures on the planet – including elephants, rhinos and giraffes. Because of this, there are many organisations working to save them.

African elephants

Once there were millions of African elephants, but today their numbers are estimated at around 700,000 and they are vulnerable to extinction. These gentle giants are very important to the grassland ecosystem. Many plants can only **germinate** once they have passed through an elephant's **digestive system**. Organisations including WWF (see page 28) work to prevent poaching, monitor populations and protect the animals' grassland home.

▼ *African elephants gather at watering holes to drink and wade to cool themselves.*

EXTREME ANIMALS

The African elephant is the world's largest land mammal, growing up to 4 m tall.

Black rhinoceros

In 1970, there were around 65,000 black rhinos in the grasslands of Africa. By 1997, there were only 2,600 left because so many had been poached for their horns. Campaigns like WWF's African Rhino Programme have been very successful, however. **Reintroduction** programmes and patrols to prevent poaching have resulted in a slow but steady rise in rhino numbers. There are now around 4,000.

Rhinos at risk

There are five **species** of rhino worldwide, and all of them are endangered. Black and white rhinos, both found in Africa's grasslands, have been the subject of **conservation** efforts. Programmes by groups including WWF, Save the Rhino and the International Rhino Foundation have all seen success in rhino conservation in Africa.

Caring for giraffes

Giraffes are classified as lower-risk animals, but their survival is dependent on conservation measures being taken to protect their habitat. The Giraffe Conservation Foundation works in Africa to make sure grassland areas are protected, to ensure a future for these graceful creatures.

▶ *Giraffes are ranked as 'conservation dependent'.*

Cats of the Savannah

Blending in among the grasses with their tawny fur, wild cats – both large and small – stalk the world's grasslands.

▲ *Tourism such as organised* **safaris** *can bring in money to help conservation efforts.*

Hunters in the grass

In Africa, big cats such as lions, leopards and cheetahs are the lords of the land. Although they have few natural predators, hunting by humans and habitat loss have put them under threat. Groups such as the African Wildlife Foundation and the Cheetah Conservation Fund work with local communities to preserve the grasslands. They also protect the cats from poaching and killing by farmers.

SAVING WILDLIFE

Lion

Although currently only listed as vulnerable by the IUCN, experts fear that lions may face a conservation crisis if steps are not taken to protect them. Their numbers have dropped from around 200,000 to just 23,000 in the past 20 years. The Born Free Foundation is one of the leading organisations for lion conservation. It has **sanctuaries** to treat injured animals. It also campaigns against hunting for sport.

EXTREME ANIMALS

Cheetahs are the fastest land animals — able to reach speeds of more than 100 km/h.

Small cats

Smaller cats such as the Geoffroy's cat, caracal, serval and African wildcat can also be found in grasslands. Caracals, found in Asia and Africa, are hunted for their fur and meat, and are often shot by farmers because they kill **livestock**. In some areas they are protected by law, but in places where they are not endangered, hunting and trade are allowed.

▶ *In the South American pampas, the small, near-threatened Geoffroy's cat is widely hunted for its fur.*

Wild Dogs and Hyenas

Many members of the dog family live in grasslands, including coyotes, African hunting dogs and maned wolves. Dog-like hyenas also roam grassland areas.

Coyote conservation

Coyotes are one of North America's greatest grassland predators. Although they are not listed by the IUCN, and can be legally hunted in the USA, there are conservation groups campaigning to make coyotes a **protected species**. The groups believe that killing animals is wrong, and that the dogs help control populations of other creatures, especially **feral** cats.

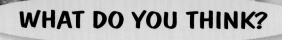

▲ *Hyenas look like wild dogs, but in fact they are more closely related to big cats. Many hyenas live on* **reserves**, *where they are protected.*

WHAT DO YOU THINK?

Hyenas are hunters and **scavengers**. They are often killed by farmers because they attack livestock. Are there some animals that it is acceptable to kill if they threaten human livelihoods? Which ones should not be killed and why?

Pampas wolves

In the South American pampas, maned wolves have come under threat because of hunting and because their habitat has been cleared to make way for farmland. There are only 1,500 maned wolves left in the wild. Organisations such as the Durrell Wildlife Conservation Trust have begun **captive-breeding** programmes to stop them dying out.

▲ Maned wolves have reddish fur and look like large foxes.

SAVING WILDLIFE

African wild dog

African wild dogs were once found in around 40 countries across the **continent**. Today their range has halved, and there are fewer than 5,500 left because of habitat loss and hunting. The African Wild Dog Conservancy in Kenya and Painted Dog Conservation in Zimbabwe work with local communities to save these endangered dogs.

▶ African wild dogs are also known as painted wolves because of the pattern on their fur.

Hoofed Animals

Swift on their feet, herds of antelope of all kinds range across the world's grasslands, as well as larger hoofed animals such as zebras and bison.

◀ *Once nearly extinct, numbers of bison are increasing again on the prairies of North America.*

WHAT DO YOU THINK?

Coyotes can kill young bison, so to save the bison, numbers of coyotes are controlled. How should we decide which animals should be saved and which killed for the benefit of other creatures?

Success on the prairies

American bison had almost died out by the start of the twentieth century. They were killed by the settlers who moved on to the prairies. The American Bison Society began to raise herds in protected reserves, and now there are around 20,000 bison.

The pronghorn antelope of the prairies is a similar success story. Conservation efforts such as controlling numbers of coyotes (the pronghorn's natural predator) mean there are now more than a million of these antelope.

African antelope

There are more than a million wildebeest – African antelope –
so they are a species of least concern to the IUCN. But numbers
are declining in countries such as Botswana because livestock
are taking over their grazing lands. People now realise that to
make sure these antelope do not become endangered, their habitat
must be carefully conserved.

▶ *Wildebeest travel
in herds across the
African plains from
Tanzania to Kenya.*

▲ *Conservation efforts may stop
numbers of Grevy's zebra falling further.*

SAVING WILDLIFE

Grevy's zebra
One type of zebra – the
quagga – is already extinct.
Now, Grevy's zebra is also
under threat. There are fewer
than 2,500, due to hunting,
habitat loss and fragmentation.
The African Wildlife
Foundation has launched the
Grevy's Zebra Research Project
to manage resources and
protected areas.

Small Mammals

Hidden among the grasses are thousands of small animals. They feed on plants and insects close to the ground, and make their homes in the earth.

Prairie dogs

Prairie dogs of North America are a key part of the grassland **food chain**, eaten by other **mammals** and birds of prey. Their current population of more than 10 million may sound high, but there were once more than a billion. People kill them because they damage crops. Local organisations campaign to have them protected, for their own sake and that of other grassland creatures.

▼ *Prairie dogs are burrowing rodents of the same animal family as squirrels.*

35 cm

Black-footed ferret

The black-footed ferret of North America was extinct in the wild by the mid-1980s because local people killed too many prairie dogs – the ferret's main food supply. Bred in captivity, hundreds have now been released back into the wild, where their numbers are rapidly increasing. They are still considered endangered, but the future looks bright.

45 cm

Mexican rabbits

Several jackrabbit species are threatened or endangered. One of the most badly affected is the Tehuantepec jackrabbit of Mexico, which is critically endangered. Its habitat has been fragmented, so it is difficult for the rabbits to find **breeding** partners. They have also been killed by fires that are deliberately started to clear the land for farming. The 1,000 remaining jackrabbits are protected by law, but this may not be enough to save them.

WHAT DO YOU THINK?

Some small mammals are killed because they are considered pests, but they can play a vital part in the food chain, being eaten by larger animals that may come under threat if this food supply disappears. How could people manage pest populations without endangering other animals?

▼ *Not all jackrabbits are endangered. The black-tailed jackrabbit is common across the grasslands of North and Central America.*

Curious Creatures

As well as being home to some of the most familiar animals on Earth, grasslands are also inhabited by some of the strangest, including anteaters, coatimundis and numbats.

Ant-eating animals

Some grassland animals are unusual because their diet consists almost entirely of ants and termites. Creatures such as aardvarks, armadillos and anteaters are ranked as least concern by the IUCN. However, experts also recognise that unless their habitat is protected, they may become endangered in the future. The giant anteater in particular is vulnerable, because it is preyed on by big cats and hunted by people for its meat and fur.

▲ *Giant anteaters of South America can reach 7 m in length, and their tongues can stretch for 60 cm to reach the ants.*

EXTREME ANIMALS

Aardvarks – mammals of the African savannah – can eat up to 50,000 ants in a day.

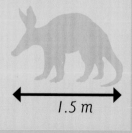

1.5 m

Coatimundis

Coatimundis, of grassland and other habitats in South America, are suffering because of human activity such as mining and road building. Although they are not currently listed as threatened, it is likely that they will face problems in the near future. Some coatimundi species have legal protection in countries such as Uruguay, but not all types are cared for in this way.

▶ *In Uruguay, white-nosed coatimundis are included on the CITES list, which controls trade in animals.*

▼ *Conservation programmes have helped increase the number of numbats in Australia's grasslands.*

SAVING WILDLIFE

Numbat

The endangered termite-eating numbat was once widespread across the grasslands and woodlands of Australia. When red foxes were introduced in the nineteenth century, though, they began killing numbats, and there are now only about 1,500 left. Captive breeding and other conservation efforts have had some success, particularly where numbats have been released back into wild areas that are free from their fox predators.

Reptiles

Animals such as snakes and lizards are always at home in long grass. It helps them to hide from their natural predators and to sneak up on their own prey.

Threatened reptiles

Grassland **reptiles** are particularly badly affected by the fires that often sweep through their habitat. Sometimes these are **wildfires**, which begin naturally, but other fires are started by humans to clear land for farming or to improve the soil. Conservation organisations work with local farming communities to limit the damage to wildlife by these fires.

Because grasslands are often close to places where humans live, some reptiles are killed out of fear by people who think they are **venomous**.

▲ *Populations of leopard tortoises are monitored and trade is carefully managed to ensure they don't become threatened.*

EXTREME ANIMALS

The black mamba of the African savannah is the deadliest snake in the world. Its venom is so powerful that it has no natural predators.

2.5 m

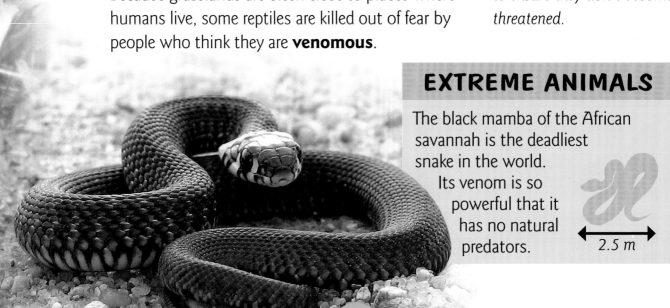

Australian lizards

Endangered grassland lizards include the pygmy blue-tongued skink and the grassland earless dragon, both of which can only be found in Australia. The changes to their environment caused by nearby farming have resulted in a decline in numbers. The Australian government has set guidelines on how people can stop these lizards becoming even more endangered, such as not grazing animals or ploughing in areas where the lizards are known to live.

▼ A large savannah monitor attacks a spitting cobra in Kenya.

1 m

SAVING WILDLIFE

Savannah monitor
The large African lizards known as savannah (or Bosc) monitors have come under threat because they are hunted for their meat, and because they are popular pets. Although they are protected by CITES, which controls international trade in endangered species, they are still traded illegally.

Minibeasts

Grasslands are alive with the sounds and movement of insects. On the ground, ants and termites scurry. In the air, flies, mosquitoes and dragonflies buzz around larger creatures at the watering holes.

▲ *Flies settle on a resting lion in the savannah.*

Ants and termites

Most insects and **arachnids** thrive in grasslands. One particularly hardy grassland insect is the nigriceps ant, which lives in whistling thorn acacias – one of the few trees that grow in the African savannah. If a grazing animal such as a giraffe tries to eat from the tree, the ants swarm out and sting it!

Across the savannah, huge mounds of earth can be seen. These are built by termites, and house **colonies** of thousands of the insects.

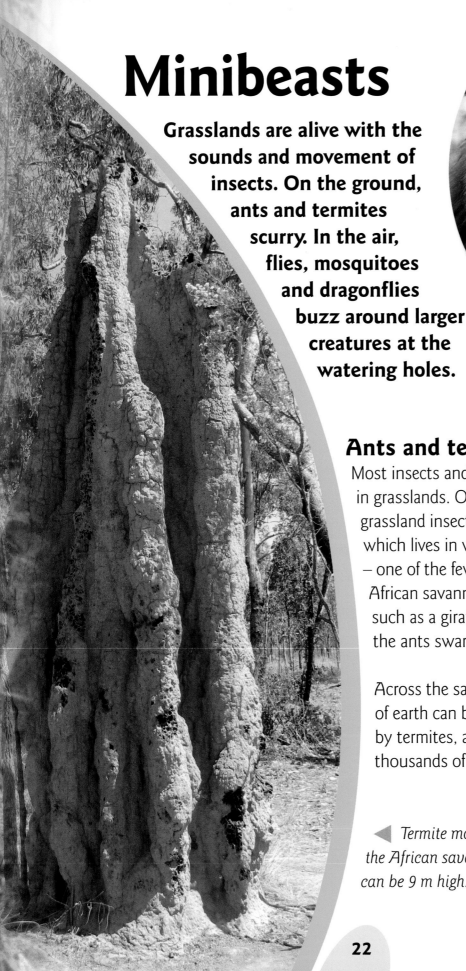

◀ *Termite mounds on the African savannah can be 9 m high.*

The importance of insects

As in many other habitats, insects play an essential part in the balance of the grassland ecosystem. They are a key food source for birds, reptiles and small mammals. Earthworms turn over the soil, allowing air to reach it and keeping it healthy. Insects such as butterflies and bees **pollinate** flowers. It is much harder to measure numbers of insects than it is larger animals, so knowing whether or not any are under threat can be difficult. However, conserving grassland habitats will make sure these important creatures continue to thrive.

▶ *A painted lady butterfly pollinates flowers on the North American prairie.*

SAVING WILDLIFE

American burying beetle

Large American burying beetles were once found all over the USA, but now loss of food sources and habitat destruction have driven them to the brink of extinction. A team from St Louis Zoo in Missouri, USA, has bred thousands of the beetles in captivity. They have been released into a reserve in Ohio, where it is hoped they will continue to thrive.

Birds on the Ground

Grasslands are home to some of the largest birds on Earth, including ostriches and emus. Some of them cannot fly, so they live, nest and breed on the ground.

Big birds

The number of ostriches in Africa has dropped dramatically in the past 100 years. Although they are not yet considered endangered, most of them only survive in game parks and reserves, where they are saved from the threats to unprotected grasslands.

In South America, rheas – birds similar to ostriches – are near threatened because their meat is popular as a food. Rhea farming and protection from international trade may stop them becoming endangered.

◀ *Many South American rheas are now raised on farms or bred in zoos to ensure their survival.*

EXTREME ANIMALS

Ostriches lay the largest eggs of any bird.

15 cm

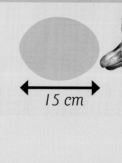

Australian emus

When Europeans first arrived in Australia they hunted emus for food, and populations declined. Now protected by law, there are more than 750,000 emus across Australia's grassland areas. However, in some parts of

▲ *Emus are the largest native birds of Australia.*

the country, wild emus are nearly extinct. Sometimes they are hit and killed by cars, but the biggest threat is loss of habitat, as people settle there.

SAVING WILDLIFE

Kakapo

Once widespread in the grassland, scrubland and forests of New Zealand, the flightless kakapo is now critically endangered. Conservation efforts, such as breeding them in reserves, have been going on since the nineteenth century, but despite this their numbers still dropped. There is now an official kakapo recovery plan, and in 2009 the total number of these birds topped 100 for the first time since the 1950s.

▲ *The kakapo is the only parrot in the world that cannot fly.*

Birds in the Air

There are not many trees in grassland areas, so birds have to find other places to nest. Sometimes they build nests on the ground, but this puts them at risk from predators such as foxes and ferrets.

Birds of prey

Birds of prey such as eagles, buzzards and vultures circle high above the world's grasslands. They can spot small mammals from far above, and will swoop in for the kill. As small creatures on the ground are endangered by fires and habitat loss, the birds have to look elsewhere for their food.

◀ *Vultures follow other animals across the grassland to feed on the remains of their prey.*

Burrowing owls nest on the ground, which makes them vulnerable to predators.

SAVING WILDLIFE

Burrowing owl

Burrowing owls of North and South America nest on the ground, usually in old burrows made by small mammals such as prairie dogs (see page 16). The owls are endangered because the prairie dogs kill them. Internationally they are listed as least concern, but in Canada they are endangered and in Mexico threatened. Conservation efforts are usually local, but most try to control habitat loss and keep down numbers of prairie dogs. Killing prairie dogs angers some people, though, as they are afraid the dogs will become endangered too.

Chickens on the brink

Prairie chickens were once common over much of North America, but like other prairie animals they have suffered from increasing human settlement. Some species are considered vulnerable, including the greater prairie chicken. In 2009, this species was declared extinct in Canada, although small groups still survive in the USA.

▶ *As people took over more prairie land for homes and farming, prairie chickens began to die out.*

What Can We Do?

Grasslands are home to some of the greatest creatures on Earth, and people work hard to save these animals and their environment. Local, national and international organisations are all involved, but there are ways that everyone can help.

Find out more...

WWF (*www.wwf.org.uk*)
This is the UK site of the largest international animal conservation organisation. On this site you can follow links to information on all sorts of endangered animals, and find out what WWF is doing to save grassland creatures.

EDGE of Existence (*www.edgeofexistence.org*)
The EDGE of Existence is a special global conservation programme that focuses on saving what it calls evolutionarily distinct and globally endangered (EDGE) species – unusual animals and plants that are under threat.

International Union for Conservation of Nature (*www.iucn.org*)
The IUCN produces the Red List, which lists all the world's known endangered species and classifies them by how under threat they are, from least concern to extinct. You can see the whole list of endangered animals on the website, as well as discover what the IUCN does to address environmental issues all over the world.

Convention on International Trade in Endangered Species (*www.cites.org*)
CITES is an international agreement between governments that aims to ensure trade in wild animal species does not threaten their survival. It lists animals that are considered to be under threat from international trading, and makes laws accordingly.

US Fish and Wildlife Service (*www.fws.gov*)
This government organisation was set up to manage and preserve wildlife in the USA. It helps manage wildlife reserves, including those in grassland regions, and makes sure laws that protect endangered animals are properly enforced.

Do more...

Sign a petition

Petitions are documents asking governments or organisations to take action on something people are concerned about. Some of the organisations opposite have online petitions that you can sign to show your support for their campaigns.

Go to the zoo

Find out if your local zoo is involved in any captive-breeding programmes and go along to find out more. Just visiting the zoo helps support these programmes.

Adopt an animal

For a small contribution to some conservation organisations you get to 'adopt' a grassland animal such as a rhino or elephant. They will send you information about your adopted animal, and keep you up to date on all the conservation efforts in the area in which it lives.

Spread the word

Find out as much as you can about the threats to grassland animals and what people are doing to save them, then tell your friends and family. The more support conservation organisations have, the more they can do!

Read more...

This is My Planet
by Jan Thornhill
(Franklin Watts, 2012)

Conservation Areas (Maps of the Environmental World)
by Jack and Meg Gillett
(Wayland, 2014)

Very Wonderful, Very Rare – Saving the Most Endangered Wildlife on Earth
by Baillie and Butcher
(Franklin Watts, 2013)

Grassland Animals Quiz

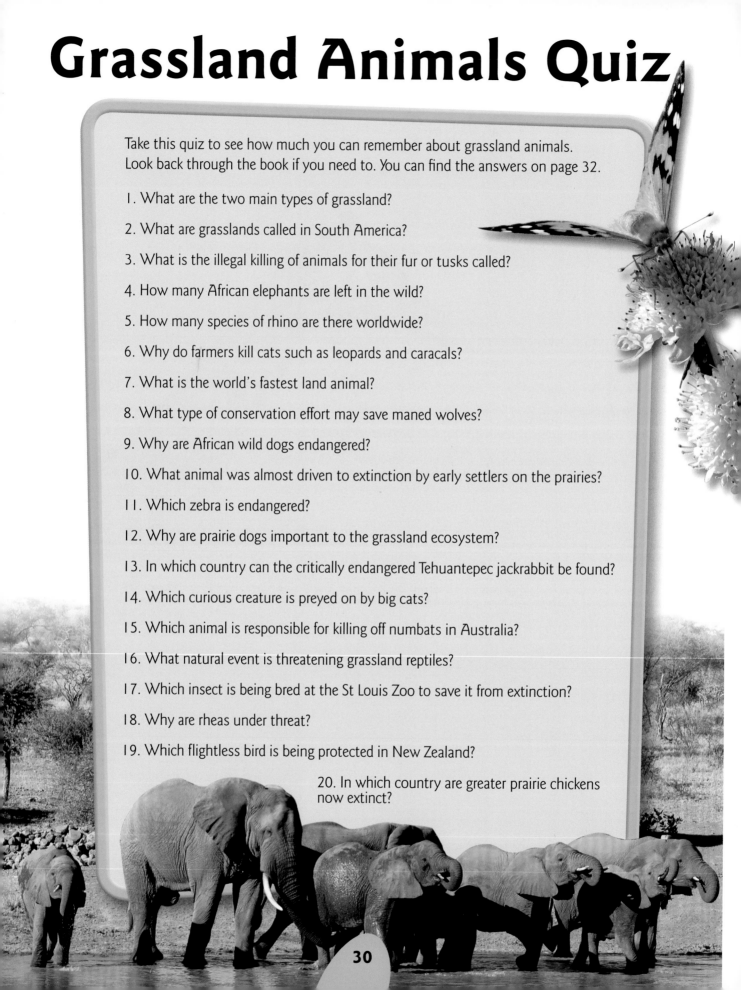

Take this quiz to see how much you can remember about grassland animals. Look back through the book if you need to. You can find the answers on page 32.

1. What are the two main types of grassland?

2. What are grasslands called in South America?

3. What is the illegal killing of animals for their fur or tusks called?

4. How many African elephants are left in the wild?

5. How many species of rhino are there worldwide?

6. Why do farmers kill cats such as leopards and caracals?

7. What is the world's fastest land animal?

8. What type of conservation effort may save maned wolves?

9. Why are African wild dogs endangered?

10. What animal was almost driven to extinction by early settlers on the prairies?

11. Which zebra is endangered?

12. Why are prairie dogs important to the grassland ecosystem?

13. In which country can the critically endangered Tehuantepec jackrabbit be found?

14. Which curious creature is preyed on by big cats?

15. Which animal is responsible for killing off numbats in Australia?

16. What natural event is threatening grassland reptiles?

17. Which insect is being bred at the St Louis Zoo to save it from extinction?

18. Why are rheas under threat?

19. Which flightless bird is being protected in New Zealand?

20. In which country are greater prairie chickens now extinct?

Glossary

arachnids creatures such as spiders and scorpions, which have eight legs.

big game large animals, such as elephants, that are hunted for sport.

breeding mating and having babies.

captive breeding when endangered animals are specially bred in zoos or wildlife reserves so that they can then be released back into the wild.

climate change a difference in the expected weather conditions or temperatures around the world.

colonies groups of animals that live and work together.

conservation efforts to preserve or manage habitats when they are under threat, or if they have been damaged or destroyed.

continent one of the Earth's seven great land masses: Africa, Antarctica, Asia, Australia, Europe, North America and South America.

digestive system the parts of the body that break down food so it can be absorbed or passed out.

ecosystem all the different types of plants and animals that live in a particular area together with the non-living parts of the environment.

endangered at risk of becoming extinct.

Equator an imaginary line around the middle of the Earth that separates the world into the Northern and Southern hemispheres.

extinct when an entire species of animal dies out, so that there are none left on Earth.

feral animals that have gone back to being wild after being domesticated.

food chain a community of plants and animals in which each is eaten by another animal.

fragmentation the breaking up of areas of land by building roads or human settlements between them.

germinate to begin to sprout or grow.

habitat the place where an animal lives.

ivory the hard, smooth substance that elephant tusks are made from.

livestock animals kept by people for meat or milk.

mammals warm-blooded animals that usually give birth to live young.

nutrients substances that help animals or plants to live and grow.

poached when an animal is hunted and killed even though it is against the law to do so.

pollinate to transfer pollen from one flower to another so that it can make seeds and grow into a new plant.

predators animals that hunt others for food.

protected species an animal that is protected by law.

reintroduction when animals that have been bred in captivity are let into the wild in areas where they once naturally occurred.

reptiles cold-blooded animals that lay eggs and usually have scales or plates on their skin.

reserves protected areas where animals can roam free and where the environment is carefully maintained for their benefit.

safaris holidays in which people are taken on a guided tour of a natural habitat, usually the African savannah, to see wild animals.

sanctuaries places where animals are protected or cared for if they are ill or injured.

scavengers animals that feed on the remains of kills left behind by other animals.

species a type of animal or plant.

venomous extremely poisonous.

wildfires fires that occur naturally but that spread quickly throughout a habitat.

Index

Numbers in **bold** indicate pictures

Quiz answers

1. Tropical and temperate; 2. Pampas; 3. Poaching; 4. 700,000; 5. Five; 6. Because they attack livestock; 7. Cheetah; 8. Captive breeding; 9. Hunting and habitat loss; 10. American bison; 11. Grevy's zebra; 12. They are a food source for other animals; 13. Mexico; 14. Giant anteater; 15. Red fox; 16. Wildfires; 17. American burying beetle; 18. They are killed for their meat; 19. Kakapo; 20. Canada.